MW01174848

A Year
in the Life
of My Son

A Year in the Life of My Son

Beth Tomkiw
Illustrated by Paula Munck

Produced by the Philip Lief Group, Inc.

Andrews McMeel
Publishing

Kansas City

99 00 01 02 03 RDC 10 9 8 7 6 5 4 3 2 1

www.andrewsmcmeel.com

ISBN: 0-7407-0037-5

Design by Holly Camerlinck

ACKNOWLEDGMENTS

Grateful thanks go to Michelle and Lori Goldman
for sparking the idea for this book.

INTRODUCTION

For a woman, a son offers the best chance to know
the mysterious male existence.

−Carole Klein

Three hundred and sixty-five days. One year. It's difficult to imagine what any boy can do with that amount of time. It can be filled with adventure. Or the mundane. It can be filled with sports. Or studies. Or girls. Baseball cards. Comic books. CDs. Starter jackets. It can be filled with hopes and dreams and longing. With success and disappointment. In short, it can brim with the full gamut of human experience. And it's up to you, dearest mom, to chronicle it. Consider this journal, *A Year in the Life of My Son*, a rare opportunity to connect with a man-child—your son, who is changing and growing every day. And, as he grows, his emotions shift . . . he may not be as comfortable expressing the way he feels about you or his family. Further, he may not be comfortable with you expressing how you feel about him. So use this journal as a means of silent expression, keeping the unspoken unspoken—but captured and expressed nonetheless.

Unlike other journals, which often cover an indefinite span of time, this one asks you to chronicle just a single year of your son's life, writing about his experiences from your point of view. Rather than wait until he's an adult, share it with him sooner—when he turns that magic thirteen (a teenager!), upon high school graduation, or "just because." The journal is organized by seasons, beginning with fall—the start of a new school year. To help prompt your prose, I've included a variety of thought starters, short statements reflecting youthful issues, interests, and challenges. But don't stop there. The "And There's More . . ." section at the end of each season allows you to recollect pages and pages worth of personal reflections, ordinary happenings, funny moments, and special events that are unique to you and your son.

I like to think of *A Year in the Life of My Son* as an opportunity to build a bridge—a bridge to more open communications. And that's the best gift you can share with your child.

A Personal Note from Me to You

Fall

Courage is being scared to death . . . and
saddling up anyway.

—John Wayne, actor

Let the School Year Begin:

Fun ways you celebrated the end of summer

_____

_____

_____

_____

_____

_____

_____

_____

_____

_____

Your grade level and what you looked forward to studying

_____

_____

_____

_____

_____

_____

_____

_____

_____

_____

_____

_____

_____

_____

_____

House of Style:

What you wore on the first day of class

_____

_____

_____

_____

_____

_____

_____

_____

_____

_____

_____

_____

_____

My thoughts on your personal style

_____

_____

_____

_____

_____

_____

_____

_____

_____

_____

_____

_____

_____

_____

_____

_____

_____

_____

_____

_____

_____

_____

_____

_____

_____

_____

_____

He's a dinosaur fanatic and is certain he wants to be a paleontologist when he grows up. Recently, he told me his chosen career would require him to live in a tent in the desert. His biggest concern? "Would you visit me, Mom?"

—Pat Todd, mother of eight-year-old Eric

Circle of Friends:

New friends you made this year

_____

_____

_____

_____

_____

_____

_____

_____

_____

_____

_____

_____

_____

_____

Old friends with whom you remain close

Like Parents, Like Son:

You reminded me of your father when . . .

_____

_____

_____

_____

_____

_____

_____

_____

_____

_____

_____

_____

_____

_____

_____

_____

_____

_____

_____

_____

_____

_____

_____

_____

The best gift I can give my children is the freedom to discover who they are—on their terms.

—Jennifer Davis, mother of sixteen-year-old Jonathan
and twelve-year-old Robert

You reminded me of myself when . . .

_____

_____

_____

_____

_____

_____

_____

_____

_____

_____

_____

_____

_____

_____

_____

_____

_____

_____

Halloween Memories:

How you spent the spookiest of holidays

_____

_____

_____

_____

_____

_____

_____

_____

_____

_____

_____

_____

_____

The tricks you played . . . and treats you enjoyed most

_____

_____

_____

_____

_____

_____

_____

_____

_____

_____

_____

_____

_____

_____

_____

_____

_____

_____

_____

_____

_____

_____

_____

_____

_____

_____

_____

_____

_____

_____

I remember very clearly, even in kindergarten or first grade, wearing black turtlenecks and walking very slowly with my hands in my pockets in the rain.

—Bret Easton Ellis, author

Never Too Old to Learn:

You taught me . . .

_____

_____

_____

_____

_____

_____

_____

_____

_____

_____

_____

_____

I don't know why women get excited over me. They didn't get excited about me when I was in high school.

—Tyson Beckford, model

_____

_____

_____

_____

_____

_____

_____

_____

_____

_____

_____

_____

_____

A challenging experience that made you grow up

_____

_____

_____

_____

_____

_____

_____

_____

_____

_____

_____

_____

_____

_____

_____

_____

_____

_____

_____

_____

_____

_____

_____

_____

_____

_____

I was never overly confident. Always nervous. Maybe I was too sheltered at home. I'm an only child and my parents were strict. It made me shy. I never raised my hand in school. I was too embarrassed to tell a girl that I had a crush on her.

—Grant Hill, athlete

Individuals who inspired you

_____

_____

_____

_____

_____

_____

_____

_____

_____

_____

_____

_____

_____

_____

_____

Heart Stopper:

I was overwhelmed when you . . .

_____

_____

_____

_____

_____

_____

_____

_____

_____

_____

_____

Moments of sheer happiness

_____

_____

_____

_____

_____

_____

_____

_____

_____

_____

_____

_____

_____

_____

_____

_____

_____

_____

_____

_____

_____

_____

_____

_____

_____

_____

_____

_____

_____

*If you live by a certain code or standard it's
not hard to decipher what's right and what's wrong. It's
simple: I have a conscience. I have to live with myself.*

—Tommy Hilfiger, designer

And There's More...

_____

_____

_____

_____

_____

_____

_____

_____

_____

_____

_____

_____

_____

_____

_____

_____

_____

_____

_____

_____

_____

_____

_____

_____

_____

_____

_____

_____

_____

_____

_____

_____

_____

Life is too short to spend what little precious time you have alive being unhappy.

—Bruce Willis, actor

Winter

*I have gone to my favorite stores, to the Laser Tag place,
to the ice-cream parlor and to the coffee place for
my favorite iced tea—it's incredible how the littlest
things in life mean the most.*

—Ike Hanson, musician

Blame It on the Weather, Part I:

Fun times you had indoors

_____

_____

_____

_____

_____

_____

_____

_____

Ways you enjoyed the rainy days or the frigid outdoors

Jolly Holidays:

Your favorite holiday gifts

_____

_____

_____

_____

_____

_____

_____

_____

_____

_____

_____

_____

_____

Thoughtful things you did for others

_____

_____

_____

_____

_____

_____

_____

_____

_____

_____

_____

_____

_____

_____

_____

Fond family moments

Friendly gatherings

Anyone who can maintain a positive attitude without much playing time earns my respect.

—Earvin "Magic" Johnson, athlete

Team Spirit:

Sports you played this year

_____

_____

_____

_____

_____

_____

_____

_____

_____

_____

There are more pleasant things to do than
beat up people.

—Muhammad Ali, athlete

Sports you enjoyed from the sidelines

_____

_____

_____

_____

_____

_____

_____

_____

_____

_____

_____

_____

_____

_____

_____

Never get to the point where you don't enjoy the game. The game is still the game. If you don't get paid a dime, you'd still play the game somewhere.

—Michael Jordan, athlete

Ways you showed good sportsmanship

Silly You:

You made me laugh when . . .

_____

_____

_____

_____

_____

_____

_____

_____

_____

_____

_____

_____

_____

Funny family moments

_____

_____

_____

_____

_____

_____

_____

_____

_____

_____

_____

_____

_____

Creative Endeavors:

Ways you expressed your artistic talents

(ruled lines for writing)

Imaginative ways you solved problems

_____

_____

_____

_____

_____

_____

_____

_____

_____

_____

_____

_____

_____

_____

_____

_____

Talk Soup:

Interesting comments you made

_____

_____

_____

_____

_____

_____

_____

_____

_____

_____

_____

_____

_____

_____

I felt guilty about being a working mom, until my son said he wanted to be a writer "just like me."

—Ellen DeVries, mother of eight-year-old Andrew

_____

_____

_____

_____

_____

_____

_____

_____

_____

_____

_____

_____

_____

_____

Things I wish we had discussed

_____

_____

_____

_____

_____

_____

_____

_____

_____

_____

_____

_____

_____

_____

It's very normal and necessary that kids listen to different music than their parents. A while ago in Germany, there was this techno wave. If everybody—parents and kids—is listening to the same music, there's something wrong.

—Richard Kruspe, musician

Wow:

A few new things I learned about you

_____

_____

_____

_____

_____

_____

_____

_____

_____

Wonderful acts of sensitivity

Under the Weather:

When you were sick, we . . .

_____

_____

_____

_____

_____

_____

_____

_____

_____

_____

_____

*What is it about men and boys? They get a cold
and they turn to mush.*

—Melissa Rhodes, mother of ten-year-old Leif

When I was sick, you . . .

_____

_____

_____

_____

_____

_____

_____

_____

_____

_____

_____

_____

_____

And There's More...

_____

_____

_____

_____

_____

_____

_____

_____

_____

_____

_____

_____

_____

_____

I don't know the key to success, but the key to failure is trying to please everybody.

—Bill Cosby, comedian and actor

Spring

I listen to motivational messages.
It helps when I hear: "I believe in me. I will move
mountains." No matter what the obstacle,
believe that you can do it.

—Tiger Woods, athlete

School Days:

Subjects that piqued your interest

_____

_____

_____

_____

_____

_____

_____

_____

Subjects that turned you off

_____

_____

_____

_____

_____

_____

_____

_____

_____

_____

_____

_____

_____

_____

_____

_____

Blame It on the Weather, Part II:

Ways you had fun when the temperature warmed

_____

_____

_____

_____

_____

_____

_____

_____

_____

_____

_____

_____

How you got through the gloomy days

_____

_____

_____

_____

_____

_____

_____

_____

_____

_____

_____

_____

_____

On a really bad day, I'll get out one of those old Chevy Chase movies, like Vacation. That guy just cracks me up. He puts an instant smile on my face.

—Matt Dillon, actor

Mood Swings:

The things that cheered you up

_____

_____

_____

_____

_____

_____

_____

_____

_____

_____

The things that bummed you out

_____

_____

_____

_____

_____

_____

_____

_____

_____

_____

_____

_____

_____

_____

_____

_____

_____

_____

_____

_____

_____

_____

_____

_____

_____

_____

_____

_____

_____

I am not the smartest or most talented person in the world, but I succeed because I keep going and going and going.

—Sylvester Stallone, actor

Silent Observations:

Impressive displays of independence

_____

_____

_____

_____

_____

_____

_____

_____

_____

_____

_____

_____

Being truthful with my kids about the mistakes
I've made has helped us build a relationship
based on honesty and trust.

—Roberta Coen, mother of fourteen-year-old Robin,
twelve-year-old Renee, and eight-year-old Evan

The times I could have helped

_____

_____

_____

_____

_____

_____

_____

_____

_____

_____

_____

_____

_____

Chores Galore:

Ways you helped around the house

_____

_____

_____

_____

_____

_____

_____

_____

_____

_____

_____

_____

Ways you could have helped more

_____

_____

_____

_____

_____

_____

_____

_____

_____

_____

_____

_____

_____

_____

I trust him; it's his hormones I worry about.

—Lisa Anne Stevens, mother of sixteen-year-old Benjamin

The Opposite Sex:

How you felt about girls

_____

_____

_____

_____

_____

_____

_____

_____

_____

_____

_____

_____

_____

_____

At first, you want someone to be beautiful, but then that really doesn't last. You have to find someone who's centered and who understands a bit about life, not just some babe who's busy being a babe.

—Nick Stabile, actor

Specific young women you liked/dated and how I felt about them

_____

_____

_____

_____

_____

_____

_____

_____

_____

_____

Dating issues that made me fret

Family Matters:

How we dealt with our differences

_____

_____

_____

_____

_____

           _____

           _____

           _____

           _____

           _____

           _____

_____

I felt bad when . . .

_____

_____

_____

_____

_____

_____

_____

_____

_____

_____

_____

_____

_____

_____

_____

_____

_____

It was fun pretending I was tough [in The Waterboy]. In real life I have no fighting skills. If you wanted to hit me, I wouldn't do anything about it. I'd just cry like a baby.

—Adam Sandler, actor and comedian

Making Impressions:

People described you as the kind of person who . . .

_____

_____

_____

_____

_____

_____

_____

The things you did when you thought no one was looking

_____

_____

_____

_____

_____

_____

_____

_____

_____

_____

_____

_____

*We were pretty ordinary kids. We just ran around on
the street, went to school, did normal stuff.
Got in our share of trouble. Typical south Texas stuff.*

—Stone Cold Steve Austin, athlete

And There's More...

Summer

Serious Business:

The things that came easy to you this year

_____

_____

_____

_____

_____

_____

_____

_____

_____

_____

_____

_____

_____

Your biggest challenges of the year

_____

_____

_____

_____

_____

_____

_____

_____

_____

_____

_____

_____

*You're talking to a guy who in a two-year span hit
every high, then lost his mother, lost his drummer—the
person he was closest to in the band—and got divorced.
Pumpkins or no Pumpkins, that's head-check time.
To have gone through that tunnel and come out the
other side—I'm happy.*

—Billy Corgan, musician

My proudest moments were when you . . .

_____

_____

_____

_____

_____

_____

_____

_____

_____

_____

_____

_____

_____

_____

_____

The things that mattered most to you this year

_____

_____

_____

_____

_____

_____

_____

_____

_____

_____

_____

_____

_____

_____

_____

_____

A Mother's Prerogative:

I worried about . . .

_____

_____

_____

_____

_____

_____

_____

_____

_____

_____

_____

_____

I changed my mind about . . .

_____

_____

_____

_____

_____

_____

_____

_____

_____

_____

_____

_____

_____

_____

_____

_____

_____

_____

When I call up my friends and complain about these grueling fourteen-hour days on the set, they're like, "Okay, shut up!"

—James Van Der Beek, actor

Working for a Living:

Ways you made money

_____

_____

_____

_____

_____

_____

_____

_____

_____

Ways you spent it

_____

_____

_____

_____

_____

_____

_____

_____

_____

_____

_____

_____

_____

He wasn't crazy about working at McDonald's—until he got his first check and was able to blow it all on concert tickets, comics, and a new pair of Airwalks.

—Anna Henley, mother of sixteen-year old Trey

Having to wake up at seven and go take the subway [to school] every morning, having to get over there with all these commuters and see every possible face of humanity and realizing that you're just the same as these other people is actually an amazingly positive thing.

—Michael "Mike D" Diamond, musician

Road Rules:

Vacation highlights . . .

_____

_____

_____

_____

_____

_____

_____

_____

_____

_____

_____

_____

_____

_____

_____

_____

_____

_____

_____

_____

_____

_____

_____

_____

_____

_____

. . . and lowlights

I actually wanted to be Dr. Dolittle. I wanted to help creatures who can't help themselves. For some reason I always felt a certain romance—platonic mind you— with animals.

—Jon Stewart, actor and comedian

Sharing:

The ways you expressed your emotions

_____

_____

_____

_____

_____

_____

_____

_____

_____

_____

How I felt when you shared your concerns

_____

_____

_____

_____

_____

_____

_____

_____

_____

_____

_____

I'd like to think he can talk to me about anything, but I realize some issues are just too private.

—Samantha Terry, mother of seventeen-year-old Blaine

How I felt when you shut me out

_____

_____

_____

_____

_____

_____

_____

_____

_____

_____

_____

_____

_____

_____

_____

_____

My father made me a soldier, and my mother gave me the strength to be one.

—Will Smith, actor and musician

Fun Times:

The year's best dances and social events

_____

_____

_____

_____

_____

_____

_____

_____

_____

_____

_____

The year's worst

_____

_____

_____

_____

_____

_____

_____

_____

_____

_____

_____

_____

_____

_____

_____

_____

And There's More...

_____

_____

_____

_____

_____

_____

_____

_____

_____

_____

_____

_____

_____

_____

_____

_____

My mom and my sister are a tough act to follow.

—Carson Daly, veejay

Some Final Reflections

I have a lot of pieces of mind [laughs]. And I'm just trying to get them together into one solid piece. A small piece. Doesn't have to be a big piece. Just my piece.

—Adam Horovitz, musician

Another Candle on the Cake:

How we celebrated your birthday

_____

_____

_____

_____

_____

_____

_____

_____

_____

Your favorite gifts

A List of Favorites:

Foods

_____

_____

_____

_____

_____

_____

_____

_____

_____

_____

_____

_____

Books

Actors and Actresses

Athletes

_____

_____

_____

_____

_____

_____

_____

_____

_____

_____

_____

_____

_____

_____

_____

_____

_____

_____

_____

Movies

_____

_____

_____

_____

_____

_____

_____

_____

_____

_____

_____

_____

_____

Don't have a cow, man.

—Bart Simpson, cartoon character

TV Shows

_____

_____

_____

_____

_____

_____

_____

_____

_____

_____

_____

_____

_____

Music

Drinks

I love my son's energy, curiosity, and sensitivity.

—Jennifer Lynn Hurley, mother of nine-year-old Josh

Dreams:

My hopes for you next year . . .

_____

_____

_____

_____

_____

_____

_____

_____

_____

_____

. . . and in the future

When I look at [my children] and see how they are, and see how people react to them, and they're so disarmingly honest and sweet and unpretentious, that's the best gift that parents could give the world, 'cause that's what we're leaving behind: [individuals] who will make a difference in the world.

—Billy Crystal, actor and comedian

_____

_____

_____

_____

_____

_____

_____

_____

_____

_____